My 23

The Lord is <u>my</u> Shepherd!

*A New Testament Perspective
on David's Classic Psalm*
Dr. Lewis W. Gregory

SOURCE

MY 23
The Lord is my Shepherd

Published by:

Source Ministries International, Inc.
PO Box 391852
Snellville, GA 30039
770-979-9804

Scripture references in this book are from the Authorized Version of The Holy Bible unless otherwise noted. The Authorized Version is considered public domain.

Cover art: original photo by Lewis W. Gregory

Dr. Gregory is President of SOURCE MINISTRIES INTERNATIONAL, INC.

SOURCE is a grace-oriented inter-denominational Christian Ministry, established in November of 1982. SOURCE is a global Christian discipleship and leadership-training ministry located in ATLANTA, GEORGIA, USA. SOURCE is committed to a grace-oriented approach to ministry based on Christ and the Cross.

http://www.sourceministries.net/go/

CONTENTS

PSALM 23

1. The LORD is my shepherd; I shall not want.
2. He makes me to lie down in green pastures: He leads me beside the still waters.
3. He restores my soul: He leads me in the paths of righteousness for His name's sake.
4. Yea, though I walk through the valley of the shadow of death, I will fear no evil: for You are with me; Your rod and Your staff they comfort me.
5. You prepare a table before me in the presence of mine enemies: You anoint my head with oil; my cup runs over.
6. Surely goodness and mercy shall follow me all the days of my life: and I will dwell in the house of the LORD for ever.

A PSALM of David

Introduction

 Scientists have discovered that your body is composed of many cells. These cells have 23 pairs of chromosomes, made of DNA, which help determine your individual identity as a human. *My 23* is about how the New Testament perspective on Psalm 23 gives you much insight into *your new identity* in union with Christ. Know yourself . . . know your God. *My 23* helps you do both.

Psalm 23 has been the "go to" chapter in the Holy Bible for centuries. Perhaps it is because of the personal details and unique description about just how caring and compassionate the Lord God Almighty is toward us. I know that this is certainly very meaningful to me.

The Lord is always on my mind. Many mornings I awake with the thought that "the LORD is my shepherd." What a great way to start the day. Thank you Lord for such a healthy reminder of whose I am and whom I serve. My identity is fixed in You and it doesn't get any better than that! Truly You are <u>my</u> shepherd!!! Psalm 23 is *my 23*.

David, the author of Psalm 23, went from one of the lowest and the least to one of the highest and greatest of all people. He became arguably the greatest king of all Israel, yeah perhaps the greatest leader of all time . . . at least until King Jesus came on the scene. What was the secret that caused David to excel in such a way? Psalm 23 gives us the answer.

7

When it comes to God, two primary questions stand out. First, is there a God? And second, can I trust Him with my life? In Psalm 23, King David, gives us a first hand account. He makes it clear that God not only exists, but that you can trust Him with your life! Knowing who the Lord is, and who you are in Him will make it possible for you to flow seamlessly through life. And that's what Jesus Christ called the abundant life! Jesus said, "I am come that you might have life, and have it more abundantly" (John 10:10). The Lord Jesus Christ is the Divine connection for abundant living. MY 23 is about this Divine connection—our relationship with the Lord made personal. MY 23 is all about the Lord, who is all about me!

The New Testament makes this clear. Jesus Christ fulfilled *The Everlasting Covenant* that God made with Abraham on behalf of all mankind. "And I will establish my covenant between me and you and your seed after you in their generations for an everlasting covenant, to be a God to you, and to your seed after you" (Genesis 17:7). The Covenant is met in Christ, and is made available to us through Him. And all the promises of God "in Christ" are yes and amen (2 Corinthians 1:20). Glory to God!

Christ, the seed of Abraham, did for us what we could not do for ourselves. He lived the perfect life, was the perfect sacrifice, in order that He might perfect that which concerns us—in a word GRACE. "And if you be Christ's, then are you Abraham's seed, and heirs according to the promise" (Galatians 3:29). According to the promise—The Everlasting Covenant —Christ makes all things new.

Therefore, the old man under sin in Adam, has been replaced by the new man under grace in Christ. Christ put the new in Covenant. Thus, "in Christ" we are made new. Through Christ we are made new creations, with new life in Christ, in order that we might walk in newness of life. This is the grace of God at work.

Thanks to The Everlasting Covenant, we are no longer under sin, we are now under grace, and recipients of everlasting LIFE in CHRIST! Jesus Christ has ushered in the new age—the age of Grace. The age of Grace is the new era of the New Creation in Christ. Hallelujah!

Therefore, let's revisit Psalm 23 from a New Testament perspective to find out more.

~1~
The Lord is <u>my</u> shepherd!

SHEPHERD

"The LORD is my shepherd." Psalm 23:1a

Shepherd! A shepherd is someone who tends to the sheep. The shepherd is responsible for the sheep. Therefore, the shepherd feels a personal responsibility for them. The Psalmist David knew only too well the role of a shepherd in regard to the sheep.

When David was a boy, he served for several years as a shepherd. He took his job very seriously; he even risked his life on several occasions for his sheep. As a shepherd, David overcame a raging lion and a ferocious bear in order to protect his sheep.

This prepared David for even greater challenges in his life. As a young man, he defeated Goliath—the most feared giant in the land. David suffered years of harassment while living as an outcast from the deranged King Saul, who wanted him dead. David not only survived, but he actually thrived amidst all these hardships. His many trials were literally "the school of hard knocks" that helped prepare him to become one of the greatest kings and champions of all times! *When the Lord is your shepherd there is advantage even in adversity.*

11

David was a man among men, a giant in his own right! It was all because of his *intimate knowledge* and *deep abiding trust* in the Lord God Almighty! Having been a shepherd, David understood quite well the responsibilities of a shepherd. As a young man tending sheep in the field alone, David had plenty of time to observe God's vast and intricate creation. He grew to love and appreciate the world around him. The concept of the LORD as a shepherd was very near and dear to David's heart. As David worked with the sheep, he began to understand who God is and what God is like.

But there is so much more to God than what David could comprehend. Therefore, God revealed Himself to us through His only begotten Son Jesus Christ. Jesus Christ is God in the flesh. He came to Earth in human form to show us more fully who God is and what God is like. Jesus compared Himself to a shepherd. *But He is no ordinary shepherd, He is the Good Shepherd.* "I am the good shepherd: the good shepherd gives his life for the sheep" (John 10:11). Jesus Christ proved that He is the Good Shepherd by willingly giving His life for us. He demonstrated His great love for His sheep when He died on the cross. "Greater love has no man than this, that a man lay down his life for his friends" (John 15:13).

David came to the realization that the Lord was *his* shepherd: his *caretaker*, his *provider*, and his *protector*. God's role as his shepherd was no idle thought. David had personally experienced this. God had constantly been there when he needed Him. It was the Lord who enabled David to overcome the lion, the bear, and the giant. David had personally seen in his own life experiences who God is and what

God can do. As a result, David was firmly convinced that *the Lord was his Shepherd!*

Psalm 23 is a foreshadowing of the Good Shepherd and our relationship to Him. This relationship was made possible as a result of Christ's fulfillment of *The Everlasting Covenant.* The Covenant between God and mankind is now complete. The Lord Jesus Christ fulfilled it through His life, His death, His burial and His resurrection. His life was paramount in preparing the way for everything else He did. He lived the perfect life, which culminated in His perfect death upon the cross. Christ walked before God, and He was perfect! This is something that neither Abraham nor any other mere human could ever possibly do (Genesis 17:1). And yet Christ did it! Therefore, His dying words were, "It is finished!"

Yes, it is finished! Mission accomplished! Christ arose from the dead and is now seated in the throne room of Heaven at the right hand of Father God. Hallelujah!!! Now, upon receiving Christ, you can be restored to God the Father. As a result, you can have a viable relationship with God because of your vital union with Christ. When you receive Christ you are born again into the family of God. God becomes your Father, and you become one of His sheep. The Lord Jesus Christ is now *your* shepherd!

So go ahead, say it, "The Lord is *my* Shepherd!!!"

"I am my beloved's, and He is mine" (Song of Solomon 6:3).

Oh Lord, the way I stumble and fumble through life, it is obvious that I need a leader—a shepherd. Therefore, I submit to your Lordship as the Shepherd of my life. I am humbled and honored that You—the Lord God Almighty, Creator of the universe—would be my Shepherd. I trust you to lead me and guide me every step of the way. Cause me to develop an intimate, personal knowledge of you. You, oh LORD, are my Shepherd!

In the name of Jesus Christ my Lord I do pray, AMEN!

~2~
The Lord is <u>my</u> shepherd!

PROVISION

"I shall not want." Psalm 23:1b

Provision! Food, clothing, and shelter may be our most basic needs, but they certainly aren't all of them. In fact, we humans are *needy people* in every respect. We want for everything!

David knew with a certainty that the Lord was the *source* and *supply* of all his needs. Furthermore, David was confident that he could trust Him with his life. Therefore, David gladly submitted himself to God as the Lord of his life. David boldly declared, "I shall not want!" There was no doubt about it, all David's needs were met in the Lord!

Likewise, all your needs are also met in the Lord Jesus Christ! Just as God committed Himself to King David, so He now has committed Himself to you in Christ. The Lord Jesus Christ is your shepherd. Jesus Himself said, I am the good shepherd and I care for my sheep. Then He proved it by giving His life for His sheep (John 10:11-13). *Christ gave Himself for us, in order that He might give Himself to us, in order that He might live His life through us.* That is pure GRACE! As a result, the Apostle Paul could confidently assert that God will supply all your needs through Christ (Philippians 4.19). Now that's "The Good Shepherd!"

15

Consider what the Good Shepherd has done for you. "He that spared not His own Son, but delivered Him up for us all, how shall He not with Him also freely give us all things?" (Romans 8:32) The New Covenant ushered in a new age—the age of GRACE for the new creation. Grace means God gives. But just exactly what has God given? He gave you Himself! He imparted His very life to you in the person of Jesus Christ. God gave you all things in Christ, so that you could do all things through Christ (Philippians 4:13). According to 2 Peter 1:3, God has given you everything you need for living life and having Godly character *in Christ.* You have everything you need in Christ. Therefore, you want for nothing!

God's order of business is simple: you seek Him and He will take care of you. He is the source of all things. All things come from Him and in Him all your needs are met. The Lord Jesus made this clear when He said, "Seek first the kingdom of God, and His righteousness; and all these things shall be added to you" (Matthew 6:33).

So who or what are you seeking? Are you trusting the Lord Jesus Christ to meet all your needs? If you are constantly *fretting* and *fearful* about how you are going to make it, then it may be because you're not fully trusting the Lord Jesus to be your shepherd. However, when you're trusting the Lord to be your shepherd, you can be satisfied anywhere, with anything. And that's pure contentment!

Then you will be able to confidently say with King David, *since the Lord is my shepherd, I shall not want.* Or, to put it another way, *because the Lord is my caretaker, I have everything I need.* And so it is, not just as a theory or a doctrine, but as a personal reality in your daily life!

So go ahead, say it, "The Lord is *my* Shepherd!!!"

"I am my beloved's, and He is mine" (Song of Solomon 6:3).

 *Dear Lord, it seems like I am always wanting something. Could it be that I have forgotten that You are my Shepherd? Cause me to realize that because You are my Shepherd, I have everything I need. Therefore, cause me to find my contentment in You and nothing else. I thank You Lord for giving me everything I need for living life and for Godly character! You, oh LORD, are my Shepherd!*

In the name of Jesus Christ my Lord I do pray, AMEN!

~3~
The Lord is <u>my</u> shepherd!

REST

"He makes me to lie down in green pastures." Psalm 23:2a

Rest! "Eat your veggies, they're good for you!" Many a parent has faced the challenge of getting their children to eat healthy foods, nutritious foods, foods that are good for them. While certain foods may not taste good to the child, the parent knows that they are good: healthy, nutritious and in the child's best interest! All good parents love their children and want what is best for them.

Likewise, the Lord God Almighty loves us—His prize creation. He is our Heavenly Father and we are His children. Therefore, He wants what is best for us. When we allow the Lord to be our shepherd, He will always do what is *best* for us. It may not always look like it or feel like it, but it is! And, if we let Him, He will take care of our physical and spiritual needs.

The "green pastures" that David mentioned are just one example of this. Such pastures are the ideal resting place for sheep. They are lush, nutritious and comfortable—the very best place for any sheep to dwell. But as any good sheep, you must follow the Good Shepherd's lead. Therefore, you must cease from your own works and allow Him to do the work through you (Hebrews 4:10). When you do, you will enter His rest—green pastures for the rest of your life! Such a peaceful, pleasant environment is your heritage "in Christ." And it will be your daily experience as you rest in Him.

God, as your loving Heavenly Father, is always looking out for your best interest. Therefore, He will give you what is best for you. He will provide you with just the right nourishment for your soul, as well as the best rest unto your soul.

I like the fact that it says, "He *makes* me." As our loving Lord, He will make sure that we get what is best for us. Sheep do not always know what is best for them, but the Good Shepherd does. And that is why He *makes* us, not to force us, but to fix us. Jesus extends this amazing offer to you, "Follow me, and I will make you" (Matthew 4:19). When you follow Christ, He will make you the best that you can be in every area of your life! And, if you wander astray, He will make sure that you get back on track. Now that is strong, decisive leadership. It is reassuring to know that under the Lord's able leadership, He will cause you to find that place of *perfect peace* and *rest!*

Jesus invites you to rest. His rest, which is a soul rest, will clear your mind, calm your emotions, and stabilize your body. The world's kind of rest is temporary and conditional. But the Lord's rest is a permanent continuous rest . . . for the rest of your life. *And He invites you to this rest with these words.* "Come unto me, all you that labor and are heavy laden, and I will give you rest. Take my yoke upon you, and learn of me; for I am meek and lowly in heart: and you shall find rest unto your souls" (Matthew 11:28-29). Come unto me. In other words, entrust your life completely to Christ, and He will take care of the rest. What a wonderful invitation!

The yoke is your resting place. The yoke is not meant to restrict you, but to liberate you: to free you to be yourself. The yoke represents Jesus Christ—the unifying factor between you and God the Father. When you are yoked to the Lord Jesus, you are joined to Him in an inseparable bond. His yoke is easy and His burden is light. The Lord becomes your burden bearer. He is here to assume the responsibility for your life. His yoke is yours for the taking.

But you must take it! So why fight it? He's on your side now. More to the point, you're on *His* side. Because of your death with Christ upon the cross, God has made you one with Him through your union with Christ. "But he that is joined to the Lord is one spirit" (1 Corinthians 6:17). You are yoked for life! The Lord is now your resting place.

Therefore, let Him take care of you. Then you can look forward expectantly to the green pastures He has prepared for you. He's your leader now, so *simply follow your Leader*. Wherever He leads, it will always be right for you. And you ultimately will find rest unto your soul. Green pastures . . . oh how refreshing. Thank you, Lord!

So go ahead, say it, "The Lord is *my* Shepherd!!!"

"I am my beloved's, and He is mine" (Song of Solomon 6:3).

Lord Jesus, it seems like I am always so busy. And the harder I try, the worse things get. I can't do it. I refuse to try anymore. I give up. I trust you with my life. I gladly take your yoke, which unites me to you. I receive your rest. Cause me to lie down in your green pastures. You are my resting place! My rest is in you Lord. You, oh LORD, are <u>my</u> Shepherd!

In the name of Jesus Christ my Lord I do pray, AMEN!

~4~
The Lord is <u>my</u> Shepherd!

PEACE

"He leads me beside the still waters."
Psalm 23:2b

Peace! In our hectic, turbulent world, we could all use some *peace* and *quiet*—a place of rest and relaxation. Still waters are just such a place: calm, quiet and relaxing. The water is nourishing and the atmosphere is soothing.

For a sheep, drinking from a stream where there is a waterfall or shoals can be very unsettling. Loud noise is often disturbing to a sheep. The deafening noise also prohibits the sheep from hearing if any possible danger is approaching. All wise shepherds understand this and lead their sheep accordingly.

As the *Good Shepherd*, our Lord Jesus Christ is acutely aware of the needs of His sheep—those who have committed their lives to Him. Therefore, He will most certainly lead us by rivers of *living water*, which are always still waters to our *soul*. Jesus said in John 7:37-39 that He would send the Holy Spirit to all those who received Him. "If any man thirst, let him come to me, and drink. He that believes on me, as the scripture has said, out of his belly shall flow rivers of living water. (But this spoke He of the Spirit, which they that believe on Him should receive.)"

Just as our bodies need physical water for physical life, so we need spiritual water for Spiritual life. The living water Jesus mentioned is a reference to the Holy Spirit. When you receive Christ, the Holy Spirit comes to live within you. At that moment Jesus Christ becomes your Lord, your life, and your all. Jesus Christ, who is the Prince of Peace, is now your peace. And to make this clear, the Lord Jesus Himself said, "These things I have spoken to you, that in me you might have peace" (John 16:33). Therefore, His peace is available to you wherever you go.

The Holy Spirit comes into your life, so that He might fill you with His presence and power. You are born of the Spirit, in order that you might be filled with the Spirit, in order that you might walk in the Spirit. When you allow the Lord to fill you with His Spirit, out of your innermost being will flow rivers of living water. Then the very character and conduct of your Lord Jesus Christ will be manifest in your life. Then His peace, which surpasses all comprehension, will permeate your being and preserve your heart and mind (Philippians 4:7). And then the peace of Christ will rule in your heart (Colossians 3:15).

Your part is simple; submit yourself to the Lord Jesus Christ as your Good Shepherd. He knows where you need to go. He also knows how you need to get there. So let the river flow. And then just go with the flow; follow His lead, and you will find peace and rest unto *your* soul!

The Lord will never lead you astray. Under His *leadership*, still waters will always be your abode, regardless of the external conditions that surround you. There may be turbulence all around you, but in your soul you will be cool, calm and collected. Now that's rest unto your soul, and peace that passes all understanding! *Still waters*—such a place exists *within your soul* because of the indwelling presence of the Spirit of the living God! Still waters are your heritage *in Christ.* Enjoy!

As you continue to drink from the wellspring of Life within you, the Spirit of the Living God will constantly refresh you. So, regardless of what comes your way, remember these words, "peace, be still" (Mark 4:39); all is well with your soul (3 John 2). Peaceful, tranquil, restful: such are the still waters of your soul. Thank you Lord for being *my* Good Shepherd!

So go ahead, say it, "The Lord is *my* Shepherd!!!"

"I am my beloved's, and He is mine" (Song of Solomon 6:3).

Lord, with all the stuff going on in my life, I could sure use some peace and quiet. I need your still waters. You are the only one who can calm my troubled soul. You are my peace. Cause the living waters of your Spirit to flow peacefully through me. I trust you to lead me by still waters. Where you lead me I will follow. You, oh LORD, are my Shepherd.

In the name of Jesus Christ my Lord I do pray, AMEN!

25

~5~
The Lord is <u>my</u> Shepherd!

RESTORATION

"He restores my soul." Psalm 23:3a

Restoration! Restoration is something everyone desperately needs. Restoration implies that something which has been damaged, broken, or destroyed needs to be made whole. As humans we're all damaged goods! First, we're defiled at conception with an evil nature by the god of this world—Satan. Then, throughout our lifetime Satan uses various means to ruin our lives and destroy our souls. Satan uses people to get to people—tormenting us in cruel and vicious ways.

As a result, our soul—with its mind, will and emotions—has been distorted, perverted and corrupted. This leaves us with a false self-image. Our perception of life and even God Himself has been skewed. Therefore, we all need restoration!

Soul-care is a God thing. You may be able to patch up your soul, dull your pain, or even modify your behavior, but it's only temporary. However, if you want a lasting cure and a permanent solution, then you need to give up on all these humanistic self-help programs. You need a total and complete restoration. That is why God sent His only begotten Son Jesus Christ to provide restoration for all mankind.

The Lord Jesus Christ is the Great Physician. He alone can restore your soul and make you whole. The Lord is here to heal your broken heart, bind up your wounded spirit, renew your mind, and restore your soul (Luke 4:18).

Are there times when you feel overwhelmed? Does each day seem to get harder and harder? Do all of your best efforts still leave you exhausted and heavy hearted? If so, then you need rest—true rest, inner rest, soul rest. Only the Lord Jesus Christ can offer a lasting solution for your life. The Lord's question for you is, "Will you be made whole?" (John 5:6)

The Lord Jesus invites you to come to Him, in order that you might find rest unto your *soul*. His yoke is easy and His burden is light (Matthew 11:28-29). When you are yoked to Him, and living out of your vital union with Him, everything becomes easy and the burdens become light. The Lord is the burden bearer. He makes the impossible possible. "With man this is impossible, but with God all things are possible" (Matthew 19:26). So go ahead, take the load off your shoulders—embrace His yoke.

Let's face it, we all have critical needs in our lives. But these needs are way beyond you. Stop trying to deny it, suppress it, or compensate for it. Only the Lord Jesus Christ Himself can restore your soul! That's what He's here for. So let Him. As you do, you will be able to relax and be yourself. And that's what *restoration* is all about!

So go ahead, say it, the Lord is *my* Shepherd!!!

"I am my beloved's, and He is mine" (Song of Solomon 6:3).

Oh Lord, I have been through so many life-shattering events. My mind is confused and my emotions are raw. I need relief! I need restoration! You are the Great Physician. Only you can make me whole. Cause your healing presence to renew my mind and restore my soul. I receive my restoration from You. Thank you for making me whole! You oh LORD are <u>my</u> Shepherd!

In the name of Jesus Christ my Lord I do pray, AMEN!

~6~
The Lord is <u>my</u> Shepherd!

RIGHTEOUSNESS

"He leads me in the paths of righteousness for His name's sake." Psalm 23:3b

Righteousness! In the *heart* of every child of God is a genuine desire to do the right thing and go the right way. However, despite the best of intentions, that does not always happen. But why not? Some would say it is simply because sheep are such dumb creatures. Although that may be true, there is so much more to it than that.

It is important to understand that good intentions are not enough! Going the right direction actually depends upon *whom* you're following. Righteousness refers to the very nature and character of God. God alone is righteous, therefore *only He* can lead us in the paths of righteousness. God's way is always the right way, and what God does is always right! *God is committed to leading us, if we'll let Him.*

How does God lead us? First of all, *He leads us to the Righteous One—the Lord Jesus Christ.* Regarding the human race we are told, "there is none righteous, no not one" (Romans 3:10). *Therefore, you must first be made right, before you can do right.* This is only possible by receiving the source of righteousness—Jesus Christ. When you do, you are made righteous in

Christ (2 Corinthians 5:21). You are made righteous, not because of any works of righteousness that you have done, but simply because of the Righteous One. The Lord is now your righteousness! (1 Corinthians 1:30)

God has a *vested* interest in you. His Son Jesus Christ died for you! And now, upon having received Christ, He indwells you. You've become one of His sheep, and He is your shepherd. Therefore, the Lord has made a commitment to lead you. What He says, He will do . . . for *His* name's sake!

So, how does the Lord lead you in the paths of righteousness on a daily basis? If you truly want to go the right way (walk in the paths of righteousness), you must have the Lord's righteous life indwelling you, and filling you. As you do, you will be led from within, by the Spirit of the Lord. To be filled with the Spirit means to be controlled by the Spirit. When you are filled with the Spirit, He will control your spirit, soul, and body. The Spirit of the Lord will guide your thoughts, rule your emotions, and motivate your will. And whatever the Lord leads you to do, He will empower, enable, and equip you to do. "For it is God who works in you both to will and to do of His good pleasure" (Philippians 2:13). The Spirit of God works within you causing you to want what He wants, and then enabling you to do what He wants. This is the *grace* of God!

Therefore, as the Spirit of the Lord prompts you, simply start walking one step at a time. If you need confirmation go to the Scriptures, and/or seek Godly counsel. But it is the still small voice of the Lord that you must heed; for He alone can lead you in the paths of righteousness! Jesus said, "My sheep hear my voice, and I know them, and they follow me" (John 10: 27). As one of His sheep, He will enable you to recognize His voice, in order that you might follow His lead.

Under *the Lord's leading*, you will always go the right way and do the right thing. He will insure that you are on the right path. But this requires a moment by moment walk of faith on your part. When you are walking in faithful obedience to your Lord, He will lead you down paths of righteousness. And such a walk always *exalts* His name. Now that's for me. Where He leads me, I will follow. I will Lord. Yes, I will! And you can too! The *paths of righteousness* await you. But you must follow His lead!

So go ahead, say it, the Lord is *my* Shepherd!!!

"I am my beloved's, and He is mine" (Song of Solomon 6:3).

Oh Lord, I have made many wrong turns and experienced numerous detours over my lifetime. I am grateful that You are my Shepherd, and that You are committed to leading me. You alone know the right path for me to take. I need Your leading in my life. Therefore, I submit to Your leadership over my life. Cause me to recognize Your voice and follow your path. I trust You to enable me to go the right way and do the right thing. You oh LORD are my Shepherd!

In the name of Jesus Christ my Lord I do pray, AMEN!

The Lord is <u>my</u> Shepherd!

PRESENCE

"Yea, though I walk through the valley of the shadow of death, I will fear no evil: for You are with me." Psalm 23:4a

Presence! The presence of evil is all around us. Evil is a clear and present danger for everyone. Dangerous and even life-threatening situations are becoming more prevalent throughout the world. No one is exempt from such calamities. Furthermore, there is often very little, if anything, we can do to prevent it. Therefore, we must always keep in mind: caution, danger ahead!

Let's face it, life can sometimes be very *fearful* and intimidating. Therefore, an undercurrent of fear and insecurity plagues many of us. To be in "the valley of the shadow of death" means that you are at *a very low point* in your life. Perhaps you even feel like you're on the brink of destruction. Or, it could be that you're living in fear of what might happen next. All of this can cause you to feel hopeless and helpless in the presence of such evil.

However, there is *an even greater presence* that is available to get you through—not just "the valley of the shadow of death," but all of life. It was this almighty presence that enabled David to rise above the presence of evil in his life. The reason that David did not fear was because he knew that *the Lord was with Him.* When David said, "You are with me" he was referring to *the Lord's presence* being with him.

Jesus took it even further when He said, "He dwells with you, and shall be in you" (John 14:17). Jesus was talking about the change that would occur as a result of His death, burial, and resurrection. Thanks to the fulfillment of the Everlasting Covenant, Christ is no longer just an external, temporal presence. Now, because of God's grace, you can become a new creation in Christ. As a result of becoming a new creation in Christ, you are now privileged to have the presence of the Lord Jesus Christ in your life. This means that Christ can now be an internal, eternal presence in your life. The Lord offers this assurance, "I will never leave you, nor forsake you. So that we may boldly say, The Lord is my [Shepherd] helper, and I will not fear" (Hebrews 13:5-6). The kind of help that the Lord offers is permanent care and protection, not just temporary assistance. Therefore, you can rest assured, your Lord is here to stay.

The Apostle Paul declared, "If God is for you, who can be against you?" (Romans 8:31) The moment you receive Christ, God is for you. Furthermore, He is never, ever against you. And since God is for you, then no one or nothing can ever be against you, not even the evil one—Satan himself. "Greater is He that is in you, than he that is in the world" (1 John 4:4). The Lord Jesus is far greater than Satan—as in no comparison. The Lord is your shield and defender. You are safe and secure in Him!

Everything changes when the *Lord God Almighty is present* in your life. God's presence makes all the difference! His presence banishes fear. The *Lord's indwelling presence* offsets every fearful situation in your life. Once you are *mindful* that the Lord is here —*no fear*.

Faith in God overcomes evil. Faith in God dispels every fear of evil. As you look beyond your fearful circumstances to your all-powerful God, you will no longer be consumed with fear. Even the worst-case scenario, the prospect of *death itself*, poses no fear because of the Lord's abiding presence. The ministry of presence is amazing; it calms your emotions, clears your mind, engages your will, and energizes you for the task at hand.

Courage, confidence and boldness are now yours in the Lord! Therefore, because the Lord is your shepherd, you can confidently say, I will fear no evil! And you won't, because of *God's* marvelous sustaining presence!

So go ahead, say it, the Lord is *my* Shepherd!!!

"I am my beloved's, and He is mine" (Song of Solomon 6:3).

Oh Lord, I have encountered many fearful circumstances in my life. And it seems like something new occurs almost every day. It is certainly beyond me. But there is nothing too hard for You. You are the Almighty God. Therefore I trust you to deliver me from evil and protect me from danger. Thank you for

making me safe and secure in You. You oh LORD are <u>my</u> Shepherd!

In the name of Jesus Christ my Lord I do pray, AMEN!

~8~
The Lord is my Shepherd!

COMFORT

"Your rod and Your staff they comfort me." Psalm 23:4b

Comfort! We all need to be comforted, and yet, we get too little of it. Even the comfort we get is not all that comforting. And it sure doesn't last very long. But then, there's a different kind of comfort—the comfort that comes from the Lord God Almighty. Now that's another story.

God's comfort is far superior to any other kind. His marvelous comfort is calming, soothing and refreshing. Most of all, it's enduring. The Lord's comfort settles and establishes us so we can get on with our lives. It makes us feel better, look better, and act better. God's comfort is good for us!

But the real comfort is found when we go astray. And that is the kind of comfort David is referring to here. It is comforting to know that even if we wander off in rebellion, disobedience, unbelief or just plain ignorance, the Lord is still there for us. He does not condemn us, abandon us, or reject us. "There is therefore now no condemnation to those who are in Christ Jesus" (Romans 8:1). Now that you are in Christ, if you fall, God is not going to put you down (condemn you). He is here to pick you up (restore

39

you). And God does not turn His back on you or leave you whenever you fall.

Jesus did not push Peter down when he began to sink under the waves in unbelief. He reached out, rescued him, and got him safely to his destination. Nothing and no one can separate us from the love of God that is in Christ Jesus our Lord (Romans 8:35-39). God may seem far away, but He never is. You are in union with Christ, and thus in an inseparable bond with Him. Therefore, there is now no separation in Christ! It should be very comforting to know that even when you fall, the Good Shepherd is always going to be there to take care of you.

How does the Lord restore us? God has many ways to restore us. Most of the time He uses His goodness. "The goodness of God leads you to repentance" (Romans 2:4). Through His goodness He will make you aware of your need of Him, as well as His care and concern for you. He will continue to lavish His goodness upon you in an attempt to woe you back. But if that does not work, then He will go to even greater lengths to restore you (Luke 15:4-6).

Desperate conditions require desperate measures. And that is where His rod and His staff come in. The Apostle Paul called this "the severity of the Lord" (Romans 11:22). Perhaps this sounds extreme to you. Maybe you're wondering, how can that be comforting? But that is the most comforting thing of all! This is not about punishment; it is about restoration. His rod and His staff are used to *protect*, *correct*, and *direct* us. They are *never* intended to harm us, but always to help us, heal us, and restore us. It may take its toll on your flesh, but it will never hurt your heart—your true self. Now that should be very comforting!

Consider the story Jesus told about the prodigal son. The son rebelled against his father. He demanded his inheritance, ran away from home and wasted away all of his father's hard earned money. Finally, in total desperation the son returned home with a repentant heart, hoping for a job among the servants. However, much to his amazement, he found his father eagerly waiting for him with open arms. His father gladly received him back, forgave him, accepted him, and restored him. Jesus told this story to illustrate the attitude that our loving Heavenly Father has toward His children when they go astray.

So, whenever God finds it necessary to apply His rod or His staff to your life, be encouraged. Welcome it! *God is looking out for you.* God's rod of reproof is for your own good. When you go astray, God's staff will get you back on track.

When you encounter the Lord's rod or His staff, always keep in mind that it is the *best* thing that could happen to you. He obviously deemed it necessary. His correction is always redemptive. Remember that the Lord is not here to hurt you, but to help you. You never need to run from the Lord for fear that He is going to harm you.

As soon as you realize the error of your ways, respond gratefully with thanksgiving, "Thanks Lord, I needed that!" Then turn to the Lord, cry out to Him, and seek Him with all your heart. That's what repentance is all about. Repentance is a change of thinking that results in a change of attitude and action. When you change your thinking and return to the Lord, He will change you, turn your life around, restore you, and make you whole again.

You have a merciful and loving Heavenly Father. He has blessed you with the Good Shepherd—the Lord Jesus Christ—to take care of you. Since the Good Shepherd loves His sheep, He will do whatever is necessary to keep you going in the right direction. And if you get off track, it is His responsibility to let you know and turn you around. "If you think otherwise, God will reveal to you the error of your ways" (Philippians 3:15NET). He will do it, first with His goodness and then with His severity, but rest assured . . . He will do it! You should *take comfort* in that! I know I do!

So go, ahead say it, the Lord is *my* Shepherd!!!

"I am my beloved's, and He is mine" (Song of Solomon 6:3).

 *Oh Lord, I have missed the mark on numerous occasions. Sometimes I find myself wandering in oblivion, headed in the wrong direction. I am so glad to know that no matter how far off course I may go, You never abandon me. It is comforting to realize that even Your rod and Your staff are designed to protect and rescue me. Therefore, I gladly accept Your correction, knowing that You want what is best for me. You oh LORD are my Shepherd!*

In the name of Jesus Christ my Lord I do pray, AMEN!

~9~
The Lord is <u>my</u> Shepherd!

SAFETY

"You prepare a table before me in the presence of mine enemies." Psalm 23:5a

Safety! Enemies are everywhere, even in your own household and among your own friends. An enemy is someone who opposes you in a harmful, negative way. We've all encountered enemies. They can be deceitful, destructive and deadly. It seems there is very little we can do about them. Or is there?

Picture yourself for a moment on a battlefield. Bullets are flying; bombs are exploding. The scene is intense! However, not all battles involve guns and bombs. Battles can occur anywhere, anytime, to anybody. The *fiery darts of destruction* come in many and varied forms. They affect us physically, mentally and emotionally. We need relief! Where are the reinforcements?

Return to the scene of battle for a moment. Do you see it? Right there in the *middle of the battlefield* is a banquet table; it is fit for a king. In fact, there's the King now. But He is not just any ordinary king, He is the King of kings—the Lord of Glory—the Lord Jesus Christ Himself. And He is seated at the head of the table, waiting just for you. He invites you to "Come and dine" (John 21:12). Wow, what an invitation!

43

A banquet table is a place where you can relax, and feast, and fellowship. But in the midst of a battlefield? No way, at least not under ordinary circumstances. But *the Lord's table* is no ordinary place. At the Lord's table, your circumstance may never change, but the Source in the midst of the circumstances changes everything. The Lord's presence in your life will permeate every area of your life, as you allow Him to fill you with His presence. And that makes all the difference. When you sit at *the Lord's table*, His presence supersedes everything else!

The Lord's table is akin to the Heavenly throne room where we are seated with Christ in the presence of Father God (Ephesians 2:6). You have the best seat in the House! So, get comfortable and relax. Relax? But in the presence of my enemies? Yes, relax! This is your safe place—in the presence of your Lord!

The safest place in a hurricane is at the very center —the eye of the storm. The turbulent, destructive winds may be whirling all around you, but the center is peaceful, calm and quiet. When the Lord Jesus Christ is central to you, and your life is centered on Him, you will be at peace wherever you go. This is true regardless of what happens, because of His presence in your life. Jesus Himself said, "In the world you shall have tribulation: but be of good cheer; I have overcome the world" (John 16:33). So cheer up! The Lord Jesus Christ is your safe place. The Lord Jesus (the overcomer) is present in you, and in Him you are an overcomer!

The Lord's presence was what enabled Moses, the leader of God's people, to face his enemies—Pharaoh and the Egyptian army. "By faith he [Moses] forsook Egypt, not fearing the wrath of the king: for he endured, as seeing Him who is invisible" (Hebrews 11:27). Moses endured, triumphed, and led God's people safely because he was aware of the Lord's presence. Moses listened to the Lord's instructions and followed His lead.

Likewise, consider Jesus. How did He handle His enemies? Some, like Judas, He allowed into His inner circle. He even gave Judas charge of the finances. Then, of all things, he allowed Judas to sit with Him at the Lord's table for the last supper. On other occasions Jesus went right into the midst of His enemies. "They got up, drove Him out of the town, and led Him to the brow of the hill on which the town was built, in order to throw Him over the cliff. But Jesus passed through the crowd and went on His way" (Luke 4:29-30). Enemies were never a threat to the Lord Jesus. Jesus instructs you to "Love your enemies, bless them that curse you, do good to them that hate you, and pray for them which despitefully use you, and persecute you" (Matthew 5:44).

Regardless of the battle that is raging in your life, you can *relax and partake* of the abundant provisions that the Lord has prepared for you. Seated at *His table* is the place of perfect peace and rest. In such a relaxed setting, with the *Lord in your midst*, your enemies are of no consequence. Just stay focused on the Lord, and what He leads you to do. He will take care of your enemies!

Your only fight is the fight of faith. But it's a good fight, because the battle has already been won! (1 Timothy 6:12) Our one true enemy—Satan—has been defeated by the Lord Jesus Christ upon the cross (Colossians 2:15). People are not your real enemy; they are only pawns in the hand of the enemy—Satan. Satan uses people to get to people, but he is the one who is the source of all death and destruction. But not to worry, Satan is a defeated foe!

Now, in union with Christ, you have victory over Satan! Therefore you are exhorted to take the stand of faith (1 John 5:4). Then, after having done all, simply stand. Stand strong in the Lord and in His mighty power (Ephesians 6:10-13). *The Lord's presence* in your life negates the presence of all your enemies. Therefore, take your place at the Lord's table, and just relax. The battle is the Lord's!

So go ahead, say it, the Lord is *my* Shepherd!!!

"I am my beloved's, and He is mine" (Song of Solomon 6:3).

Oh Lord, there are times when it seems like everyone is out to get me. Even those I considered my friends, act like enemies. Amazingly enough, right in the midst of my conflict, I discover Your presence. Thank you for granting me the best seat in the house. I am seated with you in the heavenly realm. Therefore, I am safe and secure in you. So, although I am still in the world, I'm not affected by it. Now that's the Lord's table! You oh LORD are my Shepherd!

In the name of Jesus Christ my Lord I do pray, AMEN!

~10~
The Lord is <u>my</u> Shepherd!

ENERGY

"You anoint my head with oil; my cup runs over." Psalm 23:5b

Oil! Oil is a very precious commodity. And it is even more so today due to the increasing energy demands worldwide. Therefore, oil is a valuable source of energy. Although the type of oil referred to here is somewhat different, the imagery is similar.

Oil in the Bible symbolizes the *Holy Spirit.* The Holy Spirit is God—His presence, His power, His very life. All energy comes from God. The oil of God's Spirit is the power source that is necessary to energize you. "But you shall receive power, after the Holy Spirit has come upon you" (Acts 1:8). If God's Spirit is in you, filling you to overflowing, then you will be energized for living.

So, when David referred to the Lord anointing his head with oil, it was symbolic of the Holy Spirit. To be anointed, as David described it, means that God *poured out* His Spirit upon David so that *the Lord's presence was with him.* In the Old Testament this anointing was not available to everyone. Only a few specific people, typically leaders, were chosen by God to be anointed with the Holy Spirit. These people had the Spirit with them as an *external presence,* to enable them to accomplish God's purposes.

47

However, God's intention was that we would all be able to enjoy His *indwelling presence* and power. In describing *The Everlasting Covenant* the Apostle Paul said, "You are the temple of the living God; as God has said, I will dwell in them, and walk in them; and I will be their God, and they shall be my people" (2 Corinthians 6:16). Therefore, God sent His Son Jesus Christ to prepare the way for us to have His Spirit, not just with us occasionally, but within us permanently. Jesus is called the Messiah or Christ, which means the anointed one. "God anointed Jesus of Nazareth with the Holy Spirit and with power: who went about doing good, and healing all that were oppressed of the devil; for God was with him" (Acts 10:38). *Jesus Christ is The Anointed One.*

And now because of what Christ did upon the cross, God's Spirit is readily available to everyone. You can obtain God's Spirit by *receiving* The Anointed One—the Lord Jesus Christ into your life. When you receive Christ, God *imparts* the Holy Spirit to you. At that moment you are born again of His Spirit, which makes you a new creation in Christ.

As a result of having received Christ—the Anointed One, you now have the very life of God *residing in you.* "The anointing which you have received of Him abides in you, and . . . you shall abide in Him" (1 John 2:27). Christ has made His permanent abode in you. However, many Christians do not continue to abide in Him—live in Him, by drawing their life from Him, and remaining in total dependency upon Him. Instead, they are carnal: living from the outer realm of the flesh rather than from the inner realm of the Spirit.

That is why Christ said we must abide in Him. When you are abiding in Him, your cup will be running over, because you will be filled with His Spirit. First you must "be filled with the Spirit" (Ephesians 5:18), and then you must continue to walk in the Spirit in order for the *presence and power of God* to flow through you. Being full of His Spirit always results in overflow.

It's all about *presence!* Being filled with God's continuous and inexhaustible supply insures that you will *never* run dry, no matter how draining the circumstances or demanding the task! His glorious presence and power will always preserve you and sustain you. The Spirit is God's *supernatural enablement* for living life. And now, in Him, you're fit for life!

Energy—you've got all you need in the Spirit. And in the Spirit you're empowered for living! As you *continue to yield* yourself to the Holy Spirit, you will be able to remain full to overflowing. And that powerful overflow will most certainly impact those around you with that same wonderful presence of the Lord. Thank God for *The Anointing!*

So go ahead, say it, the Lord is *my* Shepherd!!!

"I am my beloved's, and He is mine" (Song of Solomon 6:3).

Oh Lord, the demands on my life are great. At times I feel so weak and powerless. I am grateful that You are the power source. Thank you for imparting the Holy Spirit to me as my source of power. I am grateful for the anointing oil of Your presence. I yield myself completely to you. I ask you to fill me with Your Spirit. Thank You for equipping, enabling, and empowering me to live life! You oh LORD are <u>my</u> Shepherd!

In the name of Jesus Christ my Lord I do pray, AMEN!

~11~
The Lord is _my_ Shepherd!

SURELY

"Surely goodness and mercy shall follow me all the days of my life." Psalm 23:6a

Surely! David was sure and he boldly declared it. Are you sure? We all need assurance, and most of us need a lot of reassurance. It is encouraging to know that someone has our back, our front, and everything else for that matter. Life can be very challenging and very lonely. It is good to know we don't have to go it alone!

David had that kind of assurance. God's track record regarding David was excellent! God had proven His faithfulness toward David by taking care of the lion, the bear, the giant, and everything else in David's life. David was _sure and certain_ about the Lord's personal commitment to Him. God had proven it to him numerous times. And David also had a definite assurance of God's _perpetual care._

You too can have this assurance. Such assurance comes with a realization of the Lord's indwelling presence, which produces a confident certainty that you are secure in Him. He desires that your "hearts may be encouraged, having been knit together in love, and attaining to all the wealth that comes from the full assurance of understanding, resulting in a true knowledge of God's mystery, that is, Christ

Himself" (Colossians 2:2 NASB). God wants you to be encouraged with the full assurance that comes from knowing the mystery. The mystery is that once you receive Christ, Christ is in you and you are in Christ. This results in an inseparable union with Christ that joins you to the Lord. And that is your safe place! The only way you can be truly encouraged and fully united to God is to know the mystery—Christ in you. And then you will have *great assurance!*

First, *God has given us assurance* of life after death by "that Man whom He has ordained [the Anointed One Jesus Christ]; whereof He has given assurance to all men, in that He has raised Him from the dead" (Acts 17:31). Only God can give us assurance of our salvation. Upon raising Christ from the dead, God confirmed His *Everlasting Covenant* for all mankind. This assurance is proof that Jesus is the resurrection and the Life! And that's all the proof I need!

But if you need further assurance for here and now; *the Holy Spirit, who indwells you, will also reassure you.* "For our gospel came not unto you in word only, but also in power, and in the Holy Spirit, and in much assurance" (1 Thessalonians 1:5). The Holy Spirit will give you great assurance in your darkest hour. And His power will insure that you are protected and that your needs are met. He will do it!

David said God's lifetime guarantee included His goodness and His mercy. God is good; and thus God is the Source of all *goodness.* The goodness to which David referred entails everything mentioned in Psalm 23 (care, provision, rest, peace, restoration, righteousness, protection, courage, comfort, presence, power, life, fulness, assurance), and oh so much more! The "much more" according to Romans 5: 9-10, involves salvation (which insures your Heavenly life), and the saving life of Christ (which insures your present life). When you receive Christ, the source of goodness comes to indwell you. God has blessed you in Christ! "Blessed be the God and Father of our Lord Jesus Christ, who has blessed us with all spiritual blessings in heavenly places in Christ" (Ephesians 1:3). What is the blessing? Everything God is and has are now yours in union with Christ. Therefore, His goodness now accompanies you wherever you go. The Lord is *your* Shepherd, and *you are blessed!*

David goes on to speak about *mercy.* David realized that he didn't *deserve* God's gracious shepherding, or any of His goodness for that matter. After all, David had been just another dumb and wayward sheep. Haven't we all? Thankfully, it doesn't depend on our goodness. Only God is truly good! And because *God is so good,* He delights in showering His goodness upon all those who will simply *receive* it. And that's mercy, giving us what we don't deserve— His goodness, His very life. Mercy me!

You can also be a recipient of God's goodness and mercy. It begins by receiving the *source of goodness,* Jesus Christ, into your life. Then you must submit to His Lordship, so that He can lead you according to His goodness and mercy.

As you *follow the Good Lord,* His goodness and mercy will *follow you.* God offers a lifetime guarantee —His goodness and His mercy for the rest of your life. Once you've settled into the Lord as *your* Shepherd, you will have a *calm inner assurance about everything,* because you know He's looking after you. Just continue following Him, and you will *rest assured!*

So go ahead, say it, the Lord is *my* Shepherd!!!

"I am my beloved's, and He is mine" (Song of Solomon 6:3).

 *Oh Lord, with all the uncertainties in life I could use some reassurance. There are times when things seem so dark. I ask you to reassure me and encourage me by your Spirit. Cause me to know the mystery that Christ is in me. Thank you for the great assurance that you will give me by your indwelling presence. And thank you for reassuring me with your goodness and mercy! You oh LORD are my Shepherd!*

In the name of Jesus Christ my Lord I do pray, AMEN!

~12~
The Lord is <u>my</u> Shepherd!

 ## *DWELL*

"And I will dwell in the house of the Lord for ever." Psalm 23:6b

Dwell! Everyone needs a dwelling place. The "house of the Lord" that David mentioned is God's *Heavenly abode.* Heaven is the *realm* of God's eternal presence.

However, it's not just about a *place*, it's about a *person*—the Person of God Almighty, who is embodied in the Lord Jesus Christ. Therefore, the place is secondary to the person. *Heaven is where God is.* And God makes Heaven what it is—an *eternal dwelling place* of perfect peace and rest. Now that's what home is all about! And that's my kind of place!

Are you there yet? You are if you're *in Christ.* Jesus Christ is the Lord of Heaven. Regarding Heaven Jesus said, "Not everyone who says unto Me, Lord, Lord will enter the kingdom of heaven; but only the one who does the will of My Father which is in heaven" (Matthew 7:21). "For this is the will of My Father, that everyone who beholds the Son and believes in Him will have eternal life" (John 6:40). In the Heavenly Kingdom, Jesus Christ is King! God's will is clear regarding entering the Kingdom of Heaven. You must recognize that Jesus Christ is the Son of God and then believe in Him. Believing means receiving Christ into your life as your Lord and Savior. When you do, Christ comes to *dwell in you.*

You were designed by God to house Deity. "God that made the world and all things therein, seeing that He is Lord of Heaven and Earth, dwells not in temples made with hands" (Acts 17:24). God desires to dwell in temples made with His hands. *You were custom made by God to be His dwelling place.* Just think, Jesus Christ—the King of kings—wants to *dwell* in you. "That Christ may dwell in your hearts by faith" (Ephesians 3:17). Upon receiving Christ, you become His dwelling place. Christ wants to dwell in you, but He also wants you to dwell in Him, which is a faith response. You abide by faith—drawing your life from Him—and trusting Him as your life. You can remain in Christ as your life source by living in constant dependency upon Him. The result: Christ becomes your life, residing in you and living His life through. Living becomes a joint effort: you and Christ moving as one.

The fact that the King of glory has chosen to convert your humble abode into His Holy Temple is truly a mystery! "And without controversy great is the mystery of godliness" (1 Timothy 3:16). The idea that Holy God would want anything to do with sinful humanity is beyond comprehension. And yet, "God so loved the world, that He gave His only begotten Son, that whosoever believes in Him should not perish, but have eternal life" (John 3:16). God loves you and He wants you to spend eternity with Him, but He also wants you to get in on Heaven right here and now.

When you believe in Christ and receive Him into your heart, you are born again into the Heavenly Kingdom. At that moment *Heaven* comes down and glory fills your soul! Therefore, the Kingdom of Heaven, which is a spiritual kingdom, is now within you. Your body becomes God's temple, and your heart becomes His throne. And as for you, Heaven begins now, right here in this world! That is why He instructs us to pray, "Your Kingdom come. Your will be done in Earth, as it is in Heaven" (Matthew 6:10). It's time for you to begin enjoying Heaven on Earth. After all, in union with Christ you're already there!

Heaven is your heritage, both here and hereafter. "For we know that if our earthly house of this tabernacle were dissolved, we have a building of God, an house not made with hands, eternal in the heavens" (2 Corinthians 5:1). It's comforting to know that when this old body gives out, we've only just begun. And the good news is that God already has a Heavenly dwelling place awaiting us. Death is an inescapable reality. It's just a matter of time until you, as a mortal, put on immortality. Once the veil of your earthen vessel is removed, you'll discover that you've been there all along—in Heaven that is. To be absent from the body is to be present with the Lord (2 Corinthians 5:8). When your time comes to depart this Earth, you will enter His unveiled presence. Then you'll be able to see Heaven for yourself. When the veil is removed, you will see your Lord face to face. And then, you will truly worship the Lord in the beauty of His holiness! Hallelujah!!!

To be sure, Heaven is God's *exclusive* dwelling place. It's *His space*. But now, by the grace of God, you can humbly say, "Heaven is *my space* too." This is all because you are one with Christ. Christ said, "And if I go and prepare a place for you, I will come again, and receive you unto myself; that where I am, there you may be also" (John 14:3). So now, joined to the Lord of glory, you will live forever with Him in glory. We are all going to live forever, the question is where? *Therefore, to have the assurance that you will live forever in Heaven, well that's just marvelous!*

Once the Lord becomes *your Shepherd,* He will *always* remain with you. He said that He would never leave you or forsake you. He can't, because you are permanently joined together with Him. Now that's commitment—locked in for eternity! God's Everlasting Covenant has given you everlasting life, His life for ever and ever. His promise to you is sure and certain. "And, lo, I am with you always, even unto the end of the world" (Matthew 28:20). Therefore, He is with you always!

You've got a home in Heaven! It's where you belong, and it's where you will remain for all eternity! Heaven is your eternal dwelling place. David, the psalmist, understood this quite well. Therefore, he had everything to *look forward* to. But then, so do you! In Christ you're always at home, both here and hereafter. And that's a good place to be . . . always!

So go ahead, say it, the Lord is *my* Shepherd!!!

"I am my beloved's, and He is mine" (Song of Solomon 6:3).

Oh Lord, I am so grateful that You have reserved an eternal dwelling place for me. I am honored that you would make me your dwelling place. Thank You for coming to dwell in me, in order that I might dwell with You forever! I purpose to abide in You by faith, trusting you to live Your life through me. You oh Lord are my dwelling place. And You oh LORD are my Shepherd!

In the name of Jesus Christ my Lord I do pray, AMEN!

"Oh My Lord!"

Remember to acknowledge your Lord—the Good Shepherd—for all the good things He does in your daily life. The acronym "OML" will speak volumes about the Good Shepherd being your Lord. OML— Oh My Lord! Or, if you prefer, PTL— Praise the Lord! Either way, the important thing is to acknowledge Him. After all, He is your Shepherd.

In all your ways acknowledge Him, and He shall direct your paths. Proverbs 3:6

~13~
Is the Lord your Shepherd?

The First Step to Knowing God

Knowing God is the way to life!

Do you really know God? Many people think they do, when actually they only know about Him. There is far more to knowing God than merely having an intellectual knowledge of Him. What is the first step in knowing God?

1. **Admit Your Need**—Your faults, failures, bad habits and human conflicts are all indications that your need is critical. God calls such shortcomings in your life sin. "All have sinned, and come short of the glory of God" (Romans 3:23).

These sins are proof that you are a sinner. A sinner is a person with an evil nature, who is without God and therefore hopeless. Therefore, you need God.

2. **Acknowledge God's solution**—God loves you very much, and He proved it by what He did for you. He provided a solution to your problem of sin, and has a wonderful plan for your life.

His solution was to send His Son Jesus Christ to live the perfect life, and then die the perfect death on the cross for your sins. "God commends His love toward us, in that, while we were yet sinners Christ died for us" (Romans 5:8).

His plan is for you to know Him, and experience His superior quality of life. Jesus Christ explained this when He said, "I am come that they might have life, and that they might have it more abundantly" (John 10:10).

3. **Accept God's provision**—God made ample provision for all your needs through Jesus Christ. As a sinner, you do not deserve this, and there is nothing you can do to earn it. However, Jesus Christ paid the price for you through His death on the cross. Therefore, God offers this great salvation to you as a free gift.

"By grace are you saved through faith; and that not of yourselves: it is the gift of God" (Ephesians 2:8). Your part is to accept by faith what He has done for you, and receive Jesus Christ as your Lord and Savior. "As many as received Him, to them gave He power to become the sons of God, even to them that believe on His name" (John 1:12).

4. **Act on the truth**—"If you will confess with your mouth the Lord Jesus, and shall believe in your heart that God has raised Him from the dead, you shall be saved" (Romans 10:9).

If you have never done this, it is now time for you to come to know God through a personal relationship with Jesus Christ. A simple faith transaction is all that is necessary. Just direct your conversation to the one and only, invisible, yet ever present God. He is eagerly waiting for you. You may tell God something like this:

"Dear God, I admit that I am a needy person. Most of all, I need You. All my faults and failures are proof that I am a sinner. I accept the death of Jesus Christ on the cross as full payment for my sins.

I now ask You to come into my heart, Lord Jesus Christ, and take complete control of my life. I thank You for my forgiveness, and I praise You for living in me. You are now my Lord, my life, and my all!

I can do all things through Christ who is my strength. Thank You, God, for the privilege of knowing You. Amen."

If you prayed this heartfelt prayer, then you have become a Christian. The Lord is now your Shepherd, your life, your all! Congratulations! You have made an excellent decision. This is the greatest thing that could ever happen to anyone. The Lord Jesus Christ described it as being "born of the Spirit" (John 3:8).

Your new birth results in a new life. It is the Christian life, which is really the life of Christ Himself. He is now your life! You have just entered a new realm, the kingdom of God. You are now a brand new person, a child of God!

"And this is life eternal, that they might know you the only true God, and Jesus Christ whom you have sent" (John 17:3).

Knowing God is also a way of life!

And now that the LORD is your shepherd, you will be able to enjoy a whole new way of living! How? Read Introducing **The New You** by Dr. Lewis Gregory to learn more.

About the Author

Dr. Lewis W. Gregory

Dr. Lewis Gregory is an ordained minister, having been called into the ministry in 1971. He holds a Masters degree from Southwestern Baptist Theological Seminary and a Doctoral degree from Luther Rice Seminary. His ministry has been multifaceted: mission work, conference ministry, counseling, teaching, writing and the pastorate.

Lewis and his wife Lue have been married since 1969. They have three children—Amy Charis, Aaron, and Andrew—a son-in-law Rich, and a daughter-in-law Cristina and two grandchildren, Thomas and Taylor Grace Butler.

"Dr. Gregory has been wonderfully used in his ministry of preaching, teaching, and counseling here at First Baptist Church of Atlanta. We have had a number of people testify concerning how blessed they were as a result of his ministry. . . . I have had the privilege of attending one of his seminars, and can therefore personally vouch for the quality of the materials he has developed, and the effectiveness of his teaching. . . . It is my pleasure to recommend to you the ministry of Lewis Gregory." **Dr. Charles Stanley**, Pastor, First Baptist Atlanta & Founder, In Touch Ministries

http://www.sourceministries.net/go/about/ the-messenger/

About THE NEW YOU
Dr. Lewis W. Gregory

Discover a grace oriented approach to living! Christianity is so much more than rules, regulations or religious rituals. Once you become a Christian, you are a brand new person. THE NEW YOU is an in-depth look at your new life in Christ. The whole of Christianity must be redefined in light of God's amazing grace. And the results will truly amaze you! This book offers a biblically based explanation of the Christian life: what it is and how to live it.

CONTENTS

Introducing *THE NEW YOU*
About the Book

"Hey, thanks for the book! I love it. More and more people are embracing their identity in Christ. How I thank God for raising you up to preach the truth, guy! I'm proud of you."

Dr. Bill Gillham, Lifetime Guarantee Ministries, Fort Worth, TX

"I'm sure the Spirit has led you as you have worked hard for some time on this project. I'm convinced you have only one desire and that is to honor God and free humanity."

Dan Stone, former Minister, Cadiz, KY, author The Rest of the Gospel

"I appreciate the book very much and believe it will enjoy a wide ministry. Blessings on you and your fine book!"

Dr. Charles Solomon, Grace Fellowship Int'l, Pigeon Forge, TN

"The content is excellent! It is easy to read and understandable."

Dr. Frankie Rainey, Greek/N.T. Professor, Howard Payne University, Brownwood, TX

"Somewhere along my journey the simplicity and power of our union with Christ got buried beneath religion. At one time, I would have considered that to be impossible, but Introducing The New You touched those buried places and brought tears of repentance and joy all at the same time. Thank you for listening to His leading and putting the book together. Yours stays beside my chair." **JP**, TN

Discover the ultimate in Christian living.
Order a copy of this life-changing message.

Available in Hardback (325 Pages)

http://www.sourceministries.net/go/resources/the-new-you/

Available in eBook

https://www.amazon.com/Introducing-NEW-YOU/dp/B00HI13OH0/

CONTACT US

Source Ministries International
PO Box 391852
Snellville, GA 30039 USA

Phone: 770-979-9804

Email: source@integrity.com

Web: http://www.sourceministries.net/go/

Made in the USA
Middletown, DE
14 February 2022